God Painted the Hills

God painted the hills in splendor today,
He tucked every sign of Winter away,
The brown of the earth – each path that we trod
Kissed by the wonderful magic of God.

God painted the world in a beautiful green
With blue skies above and a world in between,
He touched every hilltop – each valley below
And added a sunbeam to set it aglow.

Then roses and rainbows and breezes that sigh,
So much hearts can cherish – a bright, smiling eye,
Life's lovely dreams that the heavens fulfill
Because God painted His beautiful hills.

Garnett Ann Schultz

Contents

A Shower of Blessings
from the Salesian Collection

Compiled and Edited
by Jennifer Grimaldi

Illustrated by
Robert VanSteinburg, Russell Bushée,
Paul Scully, Frank Massa,
Maureen McCarthy and Dale Begley

Dedicated to

Russell D. Bushée

whose memory
will live on
through his beautiful
works of art.

**The intent and
purpose of this volume is to
give you faith, hope and
inspiration. Hopefully it will help bring
peace and tranquility into your life. May
it be a reminder of God's love, guidance
and His many blessings.**

**Our publications help to support our work
for needy children in over 120 countries
around the world. Through our
programs, thousands of children are
fed, clothed, educated, sheltered
and given the opportunity to
live decent lives.**

Salesian Missions wishes to extend special thanks and gratitude to ou
generous poet friends and to the publishers who have given us permission to reprin
material included in this book. Every effort has been made to give prope
acknowledgments. Any omissions or errors are deeply regretted, and the publisher, upor
notification, will be pleased to make the necessary corrections in subsequent editions.

Cover photo: © Corbis/Fotosearch.com

First Edition Printed in the U.S.A. by Concord Litho Group, Concord, NH 03301.

Come Quickly, April!

Come quickly, April, and melt the snow
Which covers the path where I must go.
Awaken the crocus and daffodils,
And summon bluebirds unto the hills.
Spring forth with buds upon every tree,
And paint a bright rainbow just for me!

Awaken the rose and marigold
As clear, sunny days start to unfold,
And sprinkle the daisies with morning dew
As God resurrects everything new.
Come quickly, April, and blow me a kiss –
It just doesn't get any better than this!

Clay Harrison

*Give thanks to the Lord,
invoke His name; make known
among the nations His deeds. Sing
to Him, sing His praise, proclaim
all His wondrous deeds.*
1 Chronicles 16:8-9

It Almost Seems
Like Heaven...

When Winter's day has ended
And comes the Spring's rebirth,
It almost seems like Heaven
Is here upon the earth.

Daffodils in yellow dress,
Tulips wear colors gay,
An apple-blossom scented breeze,
The robin's roundelay.

Lilacs blooming by the gate,
Diffusing sweet perfume,
The sky above of sapphire-blue...
There is no place for gloom.

Pink flowers on a dogwood tree,
Grass sprouting fresh and green,
Shiny, dew-drenched leaves unfurled
On bush and tree are seen.

Azaleas in all their splendor
In yards 'most everywhere,
The lily's pure white bloom
That calls our hearts to prayer.

It almost seems like Heaven
Has left that bright domain
To dwell here for a season
And refresh our souls again.

Shirley Hile Powell

Why Worry?

The sun still sets
And rises at dawn,
Painting skies with color
As a new day's born.

The stars still twinkle;
The moon still glows;
The flowers still blossom;
The grass still grows.

The mountains still stand;
The seas still roll;
God's up in Heaven
Still in control.

So don't fret or worry
When troubles abound;
Sweet peace and victory
In Him are still found.

Helen Gleason

How Can You Doubt
God's Presence?

Buds appear on the trees once more,
Birds hop upon the lawn,
Days linger well into the night,
There is an early dawn.

Life is stirring everywhere,
Nests are built anew,
Folks rake up their garden beds,
Spruce up their houses, too.

The promise of eternal life,
Around us all we share,
How can you doubt God's presence
When Spring is in the air?

Ruth Moyer Gilmour

*You have made known
to me the paths of life;
You will find me with
joy in Your presence.*
Acts 2:28

A Breath
of Spring

The first buds of the season
Peek out and say, "It's time
For us to show our finery
Before we reach our prime!"

The scent of fresh-cut grass
After a gentle shower
Surpasses the finest perfume
Of each exquisite flower.

The awesome power of a tree
Conceived in a tiny seed –
Surely one of God's miracles,
Mother Nature's gift, indeed.

While harbingers of the season
Announce a new awakening,
The birds, bees and blossoms
Spring's arrival are hastening.

Gentle breezes fill the air,
Spring is peaceful and still
Waiting to end Winter's long sleep,
Its destiny to fulfill.

Erna Gwillim

But the path of the just is
like shining light, that grows
in brilliance till perfect day.
Proverbs 4:18

The Meadow and Woodland

Way out in the meadow
Where wild grasses sway
And daisies and buttercups
Bid time of day…
Where Queen Anne's lace reigns
And wild strawberries grow,
It's here one can hear
The breeze of peace blow.
Way out in the woodland
Where sun rays peep through
And pink lady's-slipper
Is fairest to view,
Here jack-in-the-pulpit
Stands straight in his spot
As if to proclaim,
"We're put here by God."
Way out in the meadow
And woodland, as well,
One finds God and Nature
Inseparable.

Loise Pinkerton Fritz

On a Hilltop

I love to sit on a hilltop
And gaze out upon the land,
To look down on God's creation
And the fruits of His loving hand.
I see some cattle grazing
In the fields so smooth and green,
As the trees add their own magic
To this warm and pastoral scene.
I see a winding little brook
Slowly flowing to and fro,
Whose riffles glisten like diamonds
Carried along on the current's flow.
I see those soft and fluffy clouds
Drifting slowly through the skies,
While I sit and quietly listen
To the birds and their mating cries.
Yes, I love to sit on a hilltop,
It brings a welcome peace to me,
To see our God's creation
The way it was meant to be.

Louis J. Kacinko

One thing I ask of the Lord; this I seek:
To dwell in the Lord's house all the days
of my life; to gaze on the Lord's
beauty; to visit His temple.
Psalm 27:4

15

The Drama of the Sea

Water, sun and sky of blue,
White-capped waves now riding high;
Sun of gold and orange hue,
Bird flocks swiftly gliding by.
Breezes whipping salted cheeks,
Sand slipping so fast away;
Bird squad silhouette in space
Against a sky of blue-tinged gray.

Now the waves are rolling fast
Like a roaring, thundering herd;
Winds rush forth to challenge them
As the voice of sea is heard.
The drama of the sea goes on
Causing wonder, reverence, awe,
With tempestuous, varied moods
Yet ruled by God's unchanging law.
Wind and ocean, sky and sun
Mingle in an awesome tryst,
Yet the sun can melt its fierceness
Changing all to docile mist.
Oh! Master of the wind and wave
And sun and sky and ocean's swell,
Our hearts cry out, "How great Thou art!
Yet in man's heart You choose to dwell!"

Helen Gleason

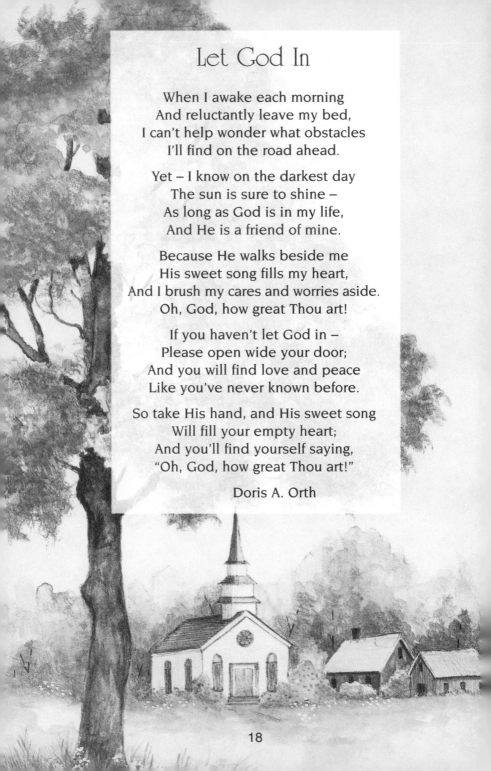

Let God In

When I awake each morning
And reluctantly leave my bed,
I can't help wonder what obstacles
I'll find on the road ahead.

Yet – I know on the darkest day
The sun is sure to shine –
As long as God is in my life,
And He is a friend of mine.

Because He walks beside me
His sweet song fills my heart,
And I brush my cares and worries aside.
Oh, God, how great Thou art!

If you haven't let God in –
Please open wide your door;
And you will find love and peace
Like you've never known before.

So take His hand, and His sweet song
Will fill your empty heart;
And you'll find yourself saying,
"Oh, God, how great Thou art!"

Doris A. Orth

Summer Interlude

The blue-sapphire skies bedazzled my eyes
And invited the clouds to go sailing.
Butterflies glide by on magical wings
On this glorious day unveiling.
Red roses were kissed by the overnight mist
That had filled their cups full of dew.
A mockingbird sang his spontaneous songs
To a golden day shining and new.
The emerald grass with daisies amassed
Stood serene in the afternoon sun.
Leaves sigh in the breeze caressing the trees
As if they would not be outdone.
I watched this display from my hushed hideaway
'Til dusk bowed to silver moonbeams,
Then I packed up my treasures and stored them inside
My trunk full of summertime dreams.

Nora M. Bozeman

*Shout joyfully to God, all you on
earth; sing of His glorious name;
give Him glorious praise.*
Psalm 66:2

A Summer Eve

Lord, how I need the quietness
Found on a Summer eve,
When sunsets are so beautiful,
And colors seem to weave
A tapestry across the sky
In shimmering shades so bold.
Soon brilliant, scarlet-crimson fades
To hues of mauve and gold.

Lord, how I need these tranquil times
As twilight shadows fall
To rest, relax and meditate,
To see Your hand in all
The good things that have come my way,
The love to me You showed.
Sometimes I take for granted, Lord,
The blessings You've bestowed.

Lord, how I need these balmy eves
When cares are laid aside
To just enjoy the quietude
And feel content inside.
The birds are singing softer now,
At dusk, a wild bird calls.
A million stars shine forth.
In peace, Your benediction falls.

Beverly J. Anderson

May the Lord give might to
His people; may the Lord bless
His people with peace!
Psalm 29:11

I Shall Return

I shall return again to what I know,
When days grow short and Autumn walks the land,
Roam the woods, and hold within my hand
A fragile dandelion, and softly blow
Its silver gray into the vale below,
Finding peace in things I understand,
Reconciled that dreams of long ago
Lie beyond the reach of any man.
When sunlight gleams upon the frost that lies
In glistening patterns on the gold and red
Of maple leaves, I shall be comforted,
Feeling tears of gladness in my eyes,
Raise my voice to hear the wind's replies
…Echo down the path that lies ahead.

Grace E. Easley

Autumn Pedestrian

Where shall I walk this Autumn day?
What shall I choose to do?
Oh, I shall wander a leafy way
Beneath a comforting blue.

I shall hug with a longing gaze
Each tree, each mellow leaf,
And wonder what lies in the distant haze
Surrounding this afternoon brief.

I shall leave worries and cares behind,
Taking along only praise;
This walk will be restful, and I will find
Peace and strength for tomorrow's days.

Where shall I wander this leafy day,
And what shall I choose to do?
Oh, I shall walk an Autumn way
And absorb an artist's view.

Pollyanna Sedziol

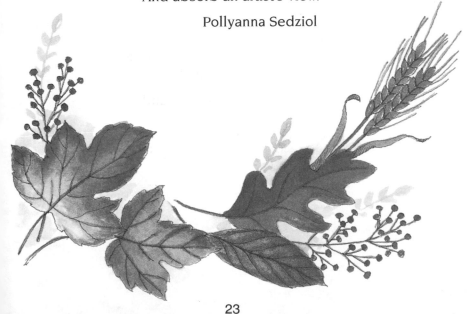

Autumn

God be with you in the Autumn
When the earth is all aglow,
As the fallen leaves of Summer
Are wind-tossed to and fro.

The frost has touched the pumpkin
And the grass is crisp and chilled.
The harvest moon is breathtaking
As it rises o'er the hill.

Apple butter bubbles thick and rich
And persimmons are ripe to eat.
Cold cider made from apples
Is a pleasant Autumn treat.

The painted hills make hearts pound.
The river runs calm and low.
Reflections of colorful trees are etched
On the water's edge below.

Smoke billows from the chimneys
And disappears high in the sky.
The wood chopper's ax lays idle
By the woodpile stacked nearby.

It's a time called Indian Summer
And my heart loves it the best.
It comes before the Winter
And it puts the Summer to rest.

Shirley Hile Powell

God's Paintbrush
in the Fall

The pathways are covered in rich design
With patterns of red, green and gold;
Trees display their exquisite color,
A breathtaking scene to behold.

The beauty we see will soon be gone,
Bright colors will fade away.
Branches will start shedding their leaves
To make way for a colder day.

But I am so grateful that I can see
The wonder of it all…
The splendor of experiencing
God's paintbrush in the Fall.

Joan Cronin Damiano

September Morning

Meadows and roadsides, brightly adorned
In shades of purple and gold,
Heart-leaved asters and goldenrod,
A beautiful sight to behold.
Butterflies frolic and dance about
In the warming rays of the sun,
While bumblebees on the nectar feast,
From flower to flower they hum.
Chirping of crickets, heard all around,
Piercing the still, fragrant air,
Their chorus grows silent, then swells again,
Crescendos erupt here and there.
Scattered white clouds drift slowly across
The deep blue Autumn sky;
Blackbirds flock to the empty fields –
How quickly has Summer gone by.

Regina Wiencek

Autumn Is So Beautiful

Autumn days are so beautiful
With foliage all aglow,
Our hearts are truly humbled
When we see such colors flow.

Maple trees take on a golden hue,
For God paints with ease and grace.
When He's finished, what a sight –
Summer's gone without a trace!

Cicadas arrive to lift each spirit
With hope before the Winter's snow,
Autumn sets hills and meadows blazing
With all the goldenrod she grows.

Each leaf that flutters by us
He has uniquely designed,
From the ginkgo's fan to the tiniest elm –
Such symmetry and line.

Sassafras and pumpkins
Prove it's autumntime upon the land,
Isn't God a wonderful Creator
That He made the earth so grand!

Linda C. Grazulis

You fixed all the limits of the earth;
Summer and Winter You made.
Psalm 74:17

Nature Awakens

Snowflakes falling on the ground,
Skaters gliding all around,
Red-nosed children on their sleds,
Soft, warm blankets on the beds.
Winter clothes are the attire,
Marshmallows roasting by the fire,
Angel figures in the snow,
Rudolph's red nose all aglow.
Trees and flowers take a rest,
Birds delay feathering nests,
Nature waits for God's command
To waken from the sleeping land.
The Creator sets the moment,
When Nature, in an instant,
Knows that wintertime is through
And all life must spring anew.

Darlene La Rose Skiff

Winter Wonder

The ermine mantle covering earth
Deftly hides the world once more
As shapes and forms begin to emerge
That have never been seen before.

Branches drip with mother-of-pearl
And diamond frost a rainbow makes
As icy castles and sparkling stars
Are mirrored in shimmering lakes.

And in this transformed magic land
Coated with soft and silent snow,
God's creatures leave a tiny trail
That vanishes into the woods below.

Eva Marie Ippolito

*As long as the earth lasts,
seedtime and harvest, cold and heat,
Summer and Winter, and day
and night shall not cease.*
Genesis 8:22

Winter

Jack Frost paints his pictures
On every windowpane,
Bare trees shake and shiver,
Tossed by wind and rain.
Snow falls heavy upon the earth
Spreading a downy sheen,
Disguising everything in Nature
Pure white instead of green.
Winter gives the earth the time
To rest from labors long,
To germinate in time for Spring
When hearts burst out in song.

Winter has its way to warm
Our lives with happiness;
It brings us Christmas – blessed day –
And a new year bound to bless –
Each and every one of us
As we live our lives in love,
Depending on our Creator – God,
To be mindful of us from above.
While Winter is with us, be not angry –
Accept it as a friend
That wraps its arms around our land,
Until it's warm again.

Sister Mary Vincentia Schroeder

Welcome to Spring

Sweep the snow
And clean the ice,
Spring is coming to town.
To Winter, Winter
We say goodbye;
Too long it's been around.
She'll dress the trees
With buds and leaves
And flower all the land.
She'll bring with her
The peepers, bees…
They'll be the springtime band.
Ready your heart
With gladsome song,
For springtime soon we'll greet.
Welcome her here,
Make her belong…
Before she takes her leave.

Loise Pinkerton Fritz

This is the day
the Lord has made;
let us rejoice
and be glad.
Psalm 118:24

It's Then I Know

When yellow daffodils appear
And nod to tulips blooming near,
When every hill and vale is green
And new leaves on the trees are seen...
When sunshine's gold is warm and bright
And bluer skies are a delight,
When showers catch us unaware
And leave a smiling rainbow fair...
When lilac scent enchants the breeze
And birds sing gayly from the trees,
When icy streams once more run free
And lend their notes of ecstasy...
When all the days are April-dressed
And hearts with renewed hope are blessed,
When there is joy abroad the earth,
It's then I know Spring's given birth!

Beverly J. Anderson

So whoever is in Christ is a
new creation: the old things
have passed away; behold,
new things have come.
2 Corinthians 5:17

Reminisce

There couldn't be a better time
To pause and reminisce,
Not about the big things,
But little things I miss.
The cardinal who built her nest
Just outside my windowpane,
The smell of fresh-turned garden earth
And the feel of warm Spring rain…

A field of bright yellow buttercups
Gracefully nodding in the breeze,
The whistles which were made for me
From the bark of a willow tree…
The scent of flowering honeysuckle
Mingled with fresh-baked bread,
The sounds of a sudden thunderstorm
And the warmth of a featherbed…
Though big things may escape me,
It's the little things I miss,
Which bring back joyful memories
When I pause to reminisce.

Ruth Harrel

Awakening

Pussy willows rub their eyes
And waken to the April skies,
Hyacinths wink at the sun
While melting snow makes rivulets run,
And robins in their brilliant vests
Become our welcome springtime guests
As hearts are warmed by sunny rays
And all's in tune on April days.

Virginia Borman Grimmer

Enter Springtime

Someone tapped at my door today
Dressed in a daffodil gown.
Her shoes were vibrant, emerald green,
The sun's golden glow was her crown.
She held a lovely, lilac bouquet
Wrapped in a blue-sapphire sky,
Tied with a glistening, dew-dropped bow
And the wind's soft, whispering sigh.
I opened my door to let her in,
Afraid she would slip away;
And that's when the balmy breezes proclaimed,
"Springtime is here today!"

Nora M. Bozeman

*The flowers appear on the earth,
the time of pruning the vines
has come, and the song of the
dove is heard in our land.*
Song of Songs 2:12

All Is Well

The virgin white of Winter
Now wears a shawl of green,
For all the trees are budding
And flowers can be seen.

The snow that chilled us yesterday
Has melted like a dream,
For now the stone is rolled away
Beneath the sunlight's gleam.

How sweet the sounds of Spring
As songbirds now return,
And here below the rainbow
Earth makes another turn.

For Spring's a noble season,
One of show and tell,
When God reveals His majesty
And shows us all is well.

Clay Harrison

Come to Me, all you who
labor and are burdened,
and I will give you rest.
Matthew 11:28

Gardeners of God

The seeds we sow are made to grow
In acts and deeds we do,
And what we harvest, in return,
Is what our efforts grew.
So, if we sow God's seeds of love –
Throughout our years of time –
The crops we harvest, every day,
Will always be divine.

It is, for us, to sow His cares
In deeds of every kind
And live the Christian way of life –
In body, heart and mind –
So we may harvest, every day,
The joys He wills to be
To gardeners of His love and care –
And Christianity.

Michael Dubina

Cast all your worries upon Him
because He cares for you.
1 Peter 5:7

God Gave Me a Garden

Each flower and leaf,
Each plant and each tree
Are miraculous treasures
The Lord gave to me.
Though I planted the seeds
In the rich, fragrant earth,
By the hand of our Lord,
They were all given birth!
Though I tended and nurtured
Each plant with such care,
Blessed by the Creator,
Each plant blossomed there.
Though I tended each flower
With patience and love,
The garden that grew
Came from Heaven above.

Elizabeth B. Delea

My Country Homeplace

Give me sweet hay barns
And windswept hollows,
White rumpled clouds laced
With the flight of swallows.

Give me fields of tall corn
In waving green rows,
And the bright orange pumpkins
That harvesttime knows.

Give me rippling creek water
Where children splash and wade
With stately oak trees lending
Cool intervals of shade.

Give me bright meadow daisies
On rolling green hills
And fruit pies cooling
On wide windowsills.

Give me these Summer miracles
In treasured beauty traced,
Where life's delights await me
In my country homeplace.

Elisabeth Weaver Winstead

He hath made everything
beautiful in His time...
Ecclesiastes 3:11

Come Summertime

My country friend, I'm thinking of you now
As Spring is brightly bursting on the bough,
And wishing I could be with you somehow
To stroll down lilac lanes that we once knew.
In our fair city, we have daffodils,
But ah, I miss God's lush green, rolling hills,
And ivy twining to the windowsills
That brought such pleasure when I was a child.
I long for country roads that slowly wend
To lilting streams that lie around the bend –
And peaceful places where a heart can mend –
Like meadows all aglow with buttercups.
For now, my friend, I'll bid a fond adieu,
Then pray that God will bless our rendezvous;
So plant an extra sunflower or two,
'Cause I'll be country-bound come summertime!

Sandra Lytle

God's Little Things...

God placed the insects on the land,
The rainbow in the sky –
He made the birds nest in the trees,
And the soaring eagle fly...

God placed the crickets in the weeds,
The flowers to crown the earth –
He made the butterflies and bees,
And filled the heavens with mirth...

God placed the rabbits in the fields,
And the fish in the sea –
He made the chipmunks and the squirrels,
And with His love blessed you and me!

Hope C. Oberhelman

Summer Beauty

The loveliness that I behold
So far beyond compare,
The joy I feel within my soul
Tells me my Savior's near.

I see Him in red roses
That bloom along the vine.
I feel Him in the gentle wind
That sweeps the Summer pines.

The sky enfolds me like a glove
Of magic azure blue,
And I'm reminded that His love
Surrounds me this way, too!

A rolling carpet of green grass
Backs up this breathless view,
And I know for me that Heaven
Will be in colors of this hue.

As the sun slips slowly out of sight
In its westerly direction,
I want to whisper, "Please don't go,
Don't end this day's perfection."

Sara Brown

Guide me in Your truth and
teach me, for You are God my Savior,
for You I await all the long day, because
of Your goodness, Lord.
Psalm 25:5

Autumn Quest

The maples wore dresses of amber and scarlet,
The sky clutched a silken shawl silver and gray,
The wind left a spicy scent trailing behind her,
And I knew at a glance it was Autumn today.
Far in the distance the cry of the blackbirds,
Winging their way over wide fields of brown,
Hazy blue wood-smoke curled up from the dry leaves,
As Autumn appeared on the outskirts of town.
And with a football light as a whisper,
Making her way over thicket and fence,
Pensively gazing with wide eyes about her,
Down went the last bar of Summer's defense.
Chancing upon her, my lonely quest ended,
And warmed by her welcome, I've followed her since.

Grace E. Easley

Autumn

There's a hint of a chill,
Autumntime has arrived,
It came in with the dawn
In a Winter's disguise.
Everyone's bundled up
And they look out of place,
Everything's still intact
With a summertime face.
Oh, I love Autumn's breeze,
There is beauty abound,
When the tinge of the leaves
Flaunts their colors around.
It's a sight to behold,
Autumntime everywhere,
One can tell by the wind
Autumn's sure in the air.

Katherine Smith Matheney

*Praise the Lord,
Who is good; God's love
endures forever...*
Psalm 136:1

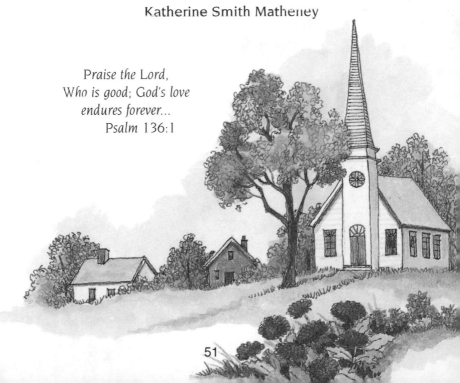

God's Glory Month

October speaks to me of God
With every phase of Autumn hue,
In flaming hills against the blue,
In waving fields of goldenrod.

No other season can compare
Or scatter, with such lavish hand,
This wealth of color o'er the land
And handiwork of God declare!

By rocky cliffs, the sparkling streams,
Wending down through wooded hills,
Or dashing through their narrow rills,
Reflect the sunlight's fading beams.

All these proclaim to eyes that see,
That beauty such as this can come
From God alone, who forms the sum
Of all created majesty!

Evelyn P. Johnston

*Yet, by my life and the Lord's
glory that fills the whole earth.*
Numbers 14:21

Autumn Messages

Autumn reminds us of God's great love
As falling leaves blanket the flowers
And birds are called to warmer climes
To sing in greener bowers –
God cares!

And it tells us of God's Fatherhood
By the yellow-gold of ripened grain,
By fruit trees heavily laden,
By crops matured by sun and rain –
God provides!

Sister Mary Gemma Brunke

Retreat Into Autumn

The tumbling leaves of Autumn
Often cause us to pause and stare,
Ocher, vermilion, and crimson,
Waltzing away all cares!

Geese in a V-formation
Squawk towards a warmer view,
While the crickets' chirping sounds endless
As if there's nothing else to do.

Goldenrods are strutting,
Scarlet sumacs join in, too,
Bright orange pumpkins suddenly appear,
So colorful they grew.

It's easy to retreat into Autumn
And thrust yourself into the beauty it gives,
Haystacks, rounded moon, shuffle of leaves –
Hurray! What a season to live.

Linda C. Grazulis

O Lord, how manifold are Thy works!
In wisdom hast Thou made them all:
the earth is full of Thy riches.
Psalm 104:24

I Love the
Autumn Best

I love the glowing days of Spring
When life is born anew,
When showers bless the April world
And flowers are blooming, too.
In Summer, fields of golden grain
Are blowing in the breeze,
And life is such a tranquil joy
With birdsong in the trees.
I love so much of God's bright world
When snowflakes gently fall,
So soft and white upon the hills –
A cover over all.

So much that ever thrills my heart
Each season of the year,
And yet the Autumn colors bright
Are always much more dear.
I love it all – the golden leaves,
Each sunset glowing red,
The colors thick and heavy there
Atop the flowerbed.
As Nature walks October trails
More precious than the rest,
Of all the seasons of our year,
I love the Autumn best.

Garnett Ann Schultz

Snow Art

Snow set into patterns by the wind
And drifted into sculptures on the hills;
White petals as of blossoms from the sky
Forming into flowers on the sills.

Enclosed within dimensions far beyond,
The breadth to which the arms of man can reach,
Close enough to touch, too far to find
Where its whiteness melts into the sea.

What hand was laid to such a tapestry
That silences all sound a little while,
Sets us free from cold anxiety
And warms us with the wonder of a child?

...Created to refresh and soothe the soul
By Winter, master artist of the snow.

Marion Weinkiper

*O*h God, how great is Thy handiwork
Of Nature's mighty works on display,
For miles of breathtaking beauty,
No pen of man could portray.
Such splendor is given to Thy landscapes,
To places both high and low,
So that great or small might behold it,
We know that our Lord planned it so.
I thank God for eyes to behold such splendor
And for a heart attuned to His own,
So I can appreciate the wonders of Autumn
Long after it has come and gone.
I thank You, God, for each season
Whichever it may be,
For I know there is beauty to be found
If only our eyes will see.
Let me not take for granted this great universe
You've given for us to enjoy and share,
We know from Your word, eye has not seen or ear heard
The joys You've prepared for us there.

Thelma Grace Ide

Open my eyes to see
clearly the wonders of
Your teachings.
Psalm 119:18

59

Springtime
in Your Heart

Keep springtime in your heart
With its healing beams of gold.
Let the fire of Autumn
Warm you through the Winter's cold.

All through the Wintry winds that blow,
When birds away have flown,
Picture rays of sunshine
Through Summers you have known.

Feel the warmth of springtime,
Let Nature's lovely sounds
Be heard again in spirit
Through all of Winter's rounds.

And when it's cold and dark
And dreary seems the day,
Bask in the warmth of God's great love
That can never pass away.

Keep springtime in your heart
Though it may seem long ago,
Through falling snow and icy winds
Its warmth in you will glow.

Spring's lovely flowers, its azure sky,
Kept fast in your mind's eye,
Will show God's love, keep hope alive
'Til Winter passes by.

Helen Gleason

Winter Memory

Childhood memory,
Gently falling snow and rain,
Cold against this little face –
Pressing on the windowpane.
Snug inside your little world,
The warmness felt within,
A shudder to the outside cold
And softly whistling wind.
A sudden chill partaken,
Seek refuge in your bed,
Then thoughts about the morrow,
A quilt pulled high above the head.

James Joseph Huesgen

Winter's Night

In moonlight glist'ning
Lie snow-covered fields,
Deep silence around,
Trees black and barren
Casting long shadows
On slumbering ground.
Stars without number
In brilliant array
Adorn the night sky,
Forever circling
In fixed constellation,
Unreachable high.
Homes in the distance
Huddled together,
Lights burning low,
Sending a message
Of warmth and contentment
Across the cold snow.

Regina Wiencek

All Things Beautiful

All things beautiful are ours,
Winter snow and springtime flowers,
Placid lakes and rushing streams,
Mountains tall, meadows green
And forests aflame in Autumn splendor,
Rare gifts of Nature God doth render.
In His great love for mankind below,
All things beautiful He doth bestow.

Kathryn Thorne Bowsher

At Winter's Call

Out my window I can see
Leaves are brown as they can be,
Though it's wintertime for sure
Dressed in finest of decor.
All seem sure to take a bow
Dancing in the wind for now,
Leaves that once belonged to Fall
Dancing brown at Winter's call.
Each are patterned and with grace,
Some look like the finest lace,
Changing colors in a while,
Seasons in the latest style.
Dancing, blowing in the wind
Leaves designed "and all by Him."
God, our Maker, up above
In His wisdom and His love.

Katherine Smith Matheney

Did You Give Thanks?

Life's little gifts that mean so much
Are strokes of friendship's velvet touch –
A loving word, a kindly deed,
A helping hand in time of need,
A bit of praise, a bit of cheer –
Small treasures that our hearts hold dear,
Did you give thanks to God today
For friendship's touch along the way?

Beverly J. Anderson

A Friend Like You

It's nice to have a friend like you
With whom my heart can share
Its little hopes and fondest dreams
Because you really care.
It's good to know I need but call
In case my foot should slip,
You're like a lighthouse in the fog
That guides my little ship.
It's nice to have a friend like you
Within this "vale of tears,"
Someone who never changes,
However long the years,
Who sees beyond the features,
And all the outward show,
And needs no words to read the thoughts
That only friends can know.
It's nice to have a friend like you,
Forever and a day,
Who through the good times and the bad,
Will never go away.
No matter what the future holds,
Whatever life may send,
I'll always know I have been blessed
…Because you are my friend!

Grace E. Easley

67

Early Spring

There's a freshness to a morning
In the very early Spring
That sets the blood to racing,
Makes hopes and plans take wing.

The crispness that's yet Winter,
The freshness that is Spring
Sets the cheeks to glowing,
Gives lips the will to sing.

The little, ice-skimmed puddles
Of the snowy melt that froze
Reflect the tints of sunrise,
The golds and pinks and rose.

And close against a great rock
Where sun's began to warm,
Are cupped some tiny blades of grass,
Safely hid from hoarfrost's harm.

I love these first Spring mornings,
Alive with hope and song,
With their whispered way of saying,
"Spring will be along!"

Almost before you know it,
She'll be dancing through the door,
Strewing hope and blossoms
Like she's always done before.

Minnie Boyd Popish

The Shadow
of God's Wings

Merciful God…
Look down from above;
Wrap us, we pray,
In Thy tender love.
Trouble and woe
Encompass us 'round;
Only in Thee
Can comfort be found.

Almighty God…
Keep watch over us;
In Thee alone
May we put our trust.
Though grief assails,
These shadows will flee,
For we've been assured
Our hope is in Thee.

Loise Pinkerton Fritz

One Day at a Time

Live one day at a time, my friend,
Soon the present will be past –
Forget those things that bother you,
And make the good things last…

Live one day at a time, my friend,
Whatever comes along –
What's past is past, just let it be,
And sing a joyful song…

Live one day at a time, my friend,
Tomorrow's yet to come –
Today is full of hope and love,
So help yourself to some…

Live one day at a time, my friend,
And happy you will be;
Relax, rejoice, and just let go,
And set your spirit free!

Hope C. Oberhelman

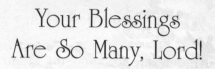

Your Blessings
Are So Many, Lord!

Your blessings are so many, Lord,
To count them one-by-one
Would take much longer than the day
That has just now begun!

You fill each day with miracles
From dawn to setting sun.
Each night You hear a million prayers
When day's work is done.

You keep this old world spinning
As seasons come and go,
And each one is a masterpiece
That sets our hearts aglow.

You fill the earth with beauty, Lord,
With flowers, shrubs and trees,
And we marvel at Your rainbows
And butterflies and bees.

Your words still give us comfort
For Your promises are true.
Your blessings are so many, Lord,
In everything we do!

Clay Harrison

Embracing Life

Some roads are rough to travel,
And through dusty trails, we've run.
We've watched as dark clouds covered skies
Abandoned by the sun.
But, anywhere we chance to be,
We know we are secure,
All surely part of God's great plan
With courage to endure.
For He has made things beautiful,
His gift is in each day.
The worth is ours for spending here,
Look up! He'll show the way.
And if we follow, God will give
A time to laugh and heal –
To make each moment meaningful,
Embracing all that's real.
We have a treasure in our lives
Worth more than any gold;
With arms outstretched, He gives His hands
For each of us to hold.

Helen M. Motti

Be a Friend Today

There always is a friend in need
Along life's lonely way;
Don't count on him to ask you,
Just be there for him today.

Just knowing there is "someone"
Is often all it takes
To lift a body's spirits
And a loyal friendship makes.

A smile, a little laughter,
A letter that you send,
Can make a world of difference
At a time one needs a friend.

An arm to proudly lean on
In times of stress or strife,
Can truly be a blessing
On the road we know as life.

Catherine Janssen Irwin

At Evening Gates

As evening gates are closing,
I stand in awe and gaze
Upon a sea of solitude
And offer up my praise.

My Lord! My God! To Thee this day
My thoughts were gratefully raised;
For in its living I was shown
The wonders of Thy works and ways.

The flora at song in my garden,
The clouds in symphonic relay,
The tides playing soulful concertos,
Were but few of the grandeurs displayed.

More graces I could not desire
Than those Thou revealest to me;
My every need I found richly fulfilled,
Free and unsparingly.

O let me be worthy of blessings
Far greater than mortals could ask;
And if Thou should will it, assign me
The lowest of one of Thy tasks...

That I might make feeble remittance
For treasures in which I have shared;
I cannot return in full payment,
No efforts to Thine may compare.

My Lord! My God! The gates grow closed,
Soon, soon shall fade the light;
But still my mind be stayed on Thee
In praise throughout the night.

Don Beckman

Blessed are you who believed
that what was spoken to you by
the Lord would be fulfilled.
Luke 1:45

Kindness

Kindness is a Christian virtue
God has willed to every heart
To enhance our life with graces
That it nurtures and imparts.
For He knows our need for kindness
In our journeys through this earth –
When we suffer strife or struggle,
Human kindness could avert.

It is, also, holy virtue –
With a double touch of grace
For the giver and receiver
To enjoy, and to embrace –
For, in giving human kindness,
We are serving Heaven's will
To be caring, unto Jesus,
And the virtues He instills.

Michael Dubina

He Makes
His Presence Known

I believe in God's existence,
For all around I see,
The beauty in the morning sun
And every greening tree.

I see Him in the ocean waves,
And when the raindrops fall,
In gently falling snowflakes,
In mountains, strong and tall.

In the laughter of a little child
Or bird that sweetly sings,
I see the God of Heaven –
He's the Lord of everything.

Mary Ann Jameson

Time

Time to watch the morning haze
Come streaming through the pane;
To see the many lovely ways
A rainbow shines through rain.

Time to feel a gentle breeze
With sunlight softly laced;
To walk through stands of poplar trees
Without a need for haste.

Time to see the great blue sky
On some September day;
To watch the clouds float softly by
As if they knew the way.

Time to hear the gentle knock
Of waves upon the sand,
Or listen at the quiet dock
Where ocean touches land.

Time to smell the sharp perfume
Of forests thick with spruce,
And find within the giant womb
A favorite blue jay roost.

Time to stand alone and dream
And feel God's peace within,
With thoughts that wander like a stream
To gather it all in.

Barbara A. McDowell

Autumn Splendor

The first bronze leaf dropped down today,
Yellow butterflies are still at play,
Through shadowed hillsides fold on fold,
The sunshine glows like cloth of gold.

Through gilded fire-thorn's tawny shade,
Maples wave leaf banners on parade.
Plump, ripe apples on orchard trees
Invite the hum of velvet bees.

On woodland trails, white birches shine,
Deep emerald tones are etched on pines,
Spry squirrels hide treasured acorns found
From towering oak to leaf-strewn ground.

Proud harvest proved a bountiful yield,
A rich cornucopia from valley and field,
Our hearts are filled with joyful praise
For God's radiant splendor of Autumn days.

Elisabeth Weaver Winstead

Mother Nature's Show

There is something enchanting about Autumn
Which stirs my very soul.
All of earth is alive with color
And the harvest moon hangs low.

The lustrous sunshine brings a warmth
As it rises o'er picturesque hills.
Night air seems to crystallize
And brings a crispy chill.

Mother Nature is most generous
To grace us with her show
Through the colorful Autumn wonder
Before the Winter's winds and snow.

Shirley Hile Powell

*Grace to you and peace from God our
Father and the Lord Jesus Christ.*
1 Corinthians 1:3

83

…Because Autumn Came

The lights are low, the house is warm,
Everyone's in bed –
I know I, too, should be asleep…
But I'll stay up instead.

The Autumn wind rattles the trees,
I shiver just a little –
For it won't be long 'til Winter's winds
Make the branches brittle.

I pull my chair up to the fire
And watch the dancing flames,
Relishing warmth and coziness…
All because Autumn came.

Tomorrow we'll rake up the leaves
Into a great big pile
And watch the kids as they jump in,
So happy all the while.

Then hot cocoa is in order
To chase the chill away,
And we'll sit around the table
To plan another day.

Oh, thank You, Lord, for the seasons
And the changes they bring!
Each happy little pleasure can
Cause the heart to sing.

I put more wood upon the fire,
Praising God's holy name –
That I can feel such contentment
…All because Autumn came.

Denise A. DeWald

What Shall I Do?

What shall I do come Autumn when
The leaves begin to fall –
To lie in wait on drowsy trails
Before the wintry call
Of whistling winds with robust throats
Which roar to auburn hills
Streaked by the brush of carmine's rouge
To wait the icy chills?
What shall I do? What shall I do
When trees grow bare, bereft?
I'll think of them as they once were
Before the Summer left
When in a green of vibrant gloss,
They swayed to graceful breeze,
But now in grip of Winter's vise,
They lose their final leaves.
And I grow sad and I grow old –
Whatever shall I do?
I'll bide my time and Spring shall come
To bring me skies of blue.

Henry W. Gurley

Autumn's an Artist

Golden leaves are rustling,
Enchantments of the Fall,
Their voices softly echo
A melancholy call.
A wisp of wind and Nature dances
To a melody so sweet,
The gardens are decorated with
Pumpkins and gourds –
Special autumntime treats!
Fall's kaleidoscope of beauty
Spins a lovely hue,
Crimson red, tangerine orange,
And a cloud-filled sky of deep blue.
The moon appears round and mellow
As it beams such a golden glow,
The earth reveals a glimpse of Heaven
When Autumn's sent below.
Truly Autumn is an artist
With a canvas brushed with color,
For this season shines a masterpiece –
Outselling all the others!

Linda C. Grazulis

The Autumntime

What could warm our hearts so much
As the Autumn of the year,
When trees have turned to red and gold
On hillsides far and near?

A gentle hush spreads o'er the land,
So peaceful and serene;
White clouds adrift on azure sky
Can get the heart to dream.

In stubbled fields of golden brown,
The harvest gathered in,
We see God's mercy and His love
Bestowed on us again.

A bluish haze on distant hills,
Wild geese in southward flight,
The sunset's flames of crimson hue,
The harvest moon so bright.

To me no other season
Could ever be so grand,
When in the Autumn of the year,
God smiles upon the land.

Kay Hoffman

Answer me, Lord, in Your generous love;
in Your great mercy turn to me.
Psalm 69:17

Life's Pattern

Life's threads all form a pattern,
Some silver, some gold.
And there are new and finer threads
To mingle with the old.

Some tiny threads are broken,
A stitch or two is skipped,
But when the work is finished,
The pattern isn't ripped.

It forms a perfect blending
Of all of life's great dreams.
With love we frame the border –
With sorrow, sew the seams.

So fold the pattern to your heart,
Sweet memories are the dearest part.

Charlotte Trevillyan Sheward

Life's Silent Times

I marvel at life's silent times
When all the world is still,
The quiet moments I so love,
My dreams I then fulfill.
The sun above is shining down
Yet never makes a sound,
The majesty of reaching fields
Where solitude abounds.
Life's silent times lend gentle peace
Just as the storm would end,
I find the miracles of life
Around the distant bend.
The earth is still – all Nature smiles
In quietness complete,
I gaze afar to friendly hills
Where earth and sky would meet.
My heart delights to snowflakes soft
That gently touch the earth,
The tender moments in the Spring
Midst magic of rebirth.
I sit alone – enjoy it all,
No hurry and no strife,
God lends me hope and faith ideal
In silent times of life.

Garnett Ann Schultz

*They found abundant and good
pastures, and the land was
spacious, quiet, and peaceful.*
1 Chronicles 4:40

Snow and Remembrance

I still feel the wonder
When mornings I would see
That o'er the night, the tranquil white
Had come to visit me.

And snow was such a special gift
When covered o'er the land,
Especially in the early morn
When touched not by a hand.

How my memories flare before me –
I still hear the joyful noise,
Playing in the falling snow,
So many girls and boys.

And snow is just for children –
They see it in such ways
That grownups cannot fathom
Though they remember yet, those days.

And as I sit here in remembrance
Within my easy chair,
There is a lad that can be had
To take my place... somewhere.

James Joseph Huesgen

Remember me, Lord, as You
favor Your people; come to me
with Your saving help.
Psalm 106:4

Snow

After Autumn comes the snow
Drifting on the scene,
To tuck a world so newly bare
To sleep in blanket, clean.

Softly, snowflakes tumble down
From darkened sky above...
Swirling, dazzling, diamond-like,
Reflecting God's pure love.

Just as snow protects the earth,
God protects each one
From straying in our lives if we
But follow His dear Son.

If we do, our lives will shine
Like softest, brightest snow,
Reflecting just a hint of Him
Who put us here to grow.

Margaret Peterson

Peaceful Night

All around darkness is falling,
Lights appear in the valley below;
The moon rises over the hillside,
Casting shadows upon the cold snow.

No breezes stir in the treetops,
The earth lies in stillness abound;
Deserted the streets and the byways;
And slowly the moon makes his round.

Regina Wiencek

With All My Love

So many times I bring You problems, Lord.
It seems my life is filled with strife and care,
And when I need someone to see me through,
I always seek Your help, dear Lord, in prayer.

But for today, I bring no problems, Lord.
I simply come to worship and to pray.
I thank You for Your never-failing love,
And for Your mercies that are new each day.

I feel Your presence in this morning hour,
A time when all the world is hushed and still.
In sweet communion, how my soul is blest.
With joy, I lift my cup for You to fill.

I bring You praise, O Lord, for all You've done,
Your faithfulness and blessings from above.
With thankfulness I offer up my gift –
A grateful heart, dear Lord… with all my love.

Beverly J. Anderson

Spring...

The trees are dressed in green again,
And glistening in the breeze;
It is that time of year again
When Spring is here to please...

The trees are dressed in green again,
And flowers are blooming bright –
It is that season of the year
That fills us with delight...

The trees are dressed in green again,
And we give thanks to God
For all the lovely things that grow
And flourish in the sod!

Hope C. Oberhelman

*Splendor and majesty go
before Him; praise and joy
are in His holy place.*
1 Chronicles 16:27

Buds of Springtime

In loveliest colors,
Springtime has arrived,
The daffodil "crocus"
Through the Winter survived.

Their beauty undaunted
By the frost of November,
Or snow-covered beds
And the cold of December.

The earth warmed by sunshine
Uncovered their faces,
And God in His wonder
Gave beauty and graces.

And buds of the springtime
Are a sight to behold,
When Winter takes off
Its coat made of cold.

Katherine Smith Matheney

*...for we walk by faith,
not by sight.*
2 Corinthians 5:7

Promises of Spring

A patch of green upon the hill,
The sweet sound of a robin's trill,
Alert me to springtime treats
That can hasten my heartbeat.
Each day is clearly brighter now
And leaves are budding on the bough,
Cute, little furry friends appear
To let me know that they're still here.
The sparkle of the babbling brook
Cannot be captured in a book,
And blooming flowers on the rise
Treat my ever-anxious eyes.
The sights and sounds of lovely Spring
To my day such joy can bring,
And I am thankful to my Lord
For beauty in such sweet accord.

Catherine Janssen Irwin

Why Worry About Tomorrow?

Why worry about tomorrow
And the rising of the sun,
Or anguish over past mistakes
That cannot be undone?
Why waste life's precious moments
On things that bruise the heart
When today is ours to fashion
Into a work of art?
Today comes but once, my friend,
It never can return –
So use it wisely while you can,
There's a lesson you may learn.
Let history record the past
And tomorrow come what may.
Be content to do your best
With what you have today!

Clay Harrison

My Unseen Guest

God walks the trail with me each day,
He is my Friend, my Guide,
However long or steep the road,
He's ever by my side.

He sits with me in evening's hush;
We speak, we laugh, we pray,
And my heart sings a joyful song…
He's never far away.

And through each dark and lonely night,
He's guarding from above.
In perfect peace, I rest secure
In His eternal love.

Lee Simmons

*You will show me the path of life,
abounding joy in Your presence, the
delights at Your right hand forever.*
Psalm 16:11

When Spring Bursts Forth...

Some believe there is no God
And would have us think it true,
But surely they must not have seen
The springtime come anew.

For who can breathe Spring's sweet perfume
Adrift on dew-drenched air
And not be drawn toward the One
Who puts the blossoms there?

Or who can hear a robin sing
While the day is yet dim
And ponder not who gives the bird
His joyous morning hymn?

Who can lift eyes heavenward
To a windswept sky of blue
Nor sense the glory of the One
Who sends the day anew?

When Spring bursts forth upon the earth
In places far and near...
Oh, who cannot believe in God
When April days are here?

Kay Hoffman

Fill us at daybreak with Your
love, that all our days we
may sing for joy.
Psalm 90:14

The Grace of God

He gives me hope and courage
To face each newborn day.
He guides me through the shadows
To light and show the way.
He comforts and sustains me
In times of my distress.
He gives me inspiration
To find true happiness.
He grants to me forgiveness
When I may go astray.
He helps me in my trials
And does my fears allay.
He never does forsake me
In moments of despair,
And when I need a helping hand,
I always find Him there.

Harold F. Mohn

His
Miraculous
Touch

Have you ever seen a rainbow...
When the sky was overcast?
Was your heart in joyous rapture
That the bloom of joy would last?
Have you e'er been blest with lightness...
And knew not from whence it came?
You could not explain the beauty...
Or the glory it contained.
Have you ever climbed a hilltop
With a grandeur view in sight?
Did you feel His presence near you?
Did you feel His sweet delight?
We have all, I'm sure, encountered
Many moments unexplained...
Like descending jewels from Heaven
With the seal in Jesus' name.
So continue on your journey
And in faith, stand firm, believe...
That His abundance will keep flowing
And in joy you will receive.

Chris Zambernard

Alone in Quietude

When I'm alone in quietude
Near ending of the day
And sunlight tiptoes through the room
And children cease their play,
'Tis then I pause and find the time
To listen with my heart
To all the things God has to say –
To wisdom He'll impart.

I watch the shadows as they creep
So lazily along;
Outside the birds are seeking roost
And hush their evening song.

The languid sun faints in the west –
I feel the evening breeze
While stars begin to dot the sky
And darkness sifts through trees.

The stillness of the evening is
A time to kneel in prayer
And thank our Heavenly Father for
His never-ending care.
To God I'm ever grateful that
He ne'er forsakes us here;
Oh Jesus, blest Redeemer,
Your name, I hold most dear!

Luther Elvis Albright

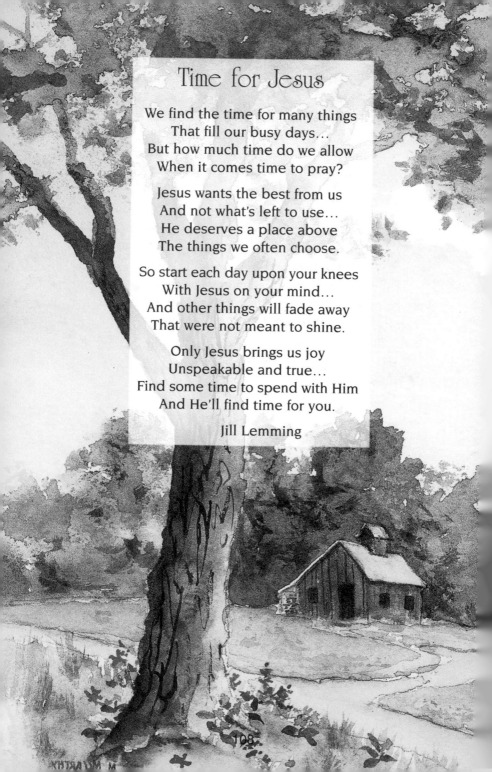

Time for Jesus

We find the time for many things
That fill our busy days…
But how much time do we allow
When it comes time to pray?

Jesus wants the best from us
And not what's left to use…
He deserves a place above
The things we often choose.

So start each day upon your knees
With Jesus on your mind…
And other things will fade away
That were not meant to shine.

Only Jesus brings us joy
Unspeakable and true…
Find some time to spend with Him
And He'll find time for you.

Jill Lemming

Our Dwelling Place

How lovely is our dwelling place,
That God has made to be:
An earth of love and thrills and joys
And dwells of ecstacy,
And we are blessed – in every hour –
To simply look to find
These glories that He made for us,
To grace our heart and mind

He touched with grace all common things
That we must see each day
And molded majesties of art
To bless our traveling ways.
A million gifts of love and peace
He blessed upon this earth
To make our life and dwelling place
A joy of Christian worth.

Michael Dubina

Teach Me To Go Slow

Teach me to go slow, Lord,
And learn to wait on You –
Don't let me jump ahead
While wondering what to do.

Teach me to go slow, Lord;
Each promise You'll fulfill –
You answer in Your time
And in Your perfect will.

Teach me to go slow, Lord,
And calm my anxious heart;
Keep my eyes on You and
Don't let the teardrops start.

Teach me to go slow, Lord,
Reach out and take my hand –
For I am deeply troubled
And just don't understand.

Teach me to go slow, Lord;
Take one day at a time –
Don't let me fall, but lead me on
To peaceful heights sublime.

Teach me to go slow, Lord,
Please work this out for me –
When all is right once more,
Let me give praise to Thee.

Teach me to go slow, Lord,
And help me see above
This dark cloud till I can gaze…
Into Your face of love.

Denise A. DeWald

Faithful Child of God

Oh, child of God, look upward,
Look toward the heavens bright.
Whenever you're discouraged,
Look to the Father of lights.
Trouble-filled is this old world;
It's oft so dark and drear,
But God is just a prayer away,
Your every prayer He'll hear.

Set your heart on things above,
Oh, faithful child of God;
Let not rumblings of this world
Be like a darkened cloud.
Think on just and honest things,
The lovely and the pure;
Submit your being to the Lord,
He'll comfort and assure.

Loise Pinkerton Fritz

114

Gifts of Autumn

Autumn brings us misty mornings
With a crispness in the air,
Sapphire-blue skies shining brightly
And a brilliance everywhere.
Autumn brings us painted hillsides
With their foliage all ablaze –
Reds and yellow, scarlet, amber
Set against a purple haze.
Autumn brings us crimson maples,
Aspens that are gowned in gold,
Evergreens that lend their color –
All a beauty to behold!
Autumn brings us mums and asters,
Goldenrod and cattails tall,
Frosty evenings, warmth of fireside,
Full moon that gold-glimmers all.
Autumn brings us fruitful harvest,
Lavish bounty of the land,
Blessings with each day unfolding –
Gifts from God's all gracious hand.

Beverly J. Anderson

Give to the Lord
the glory due His Name!
Bring gifts and enter
His courts.
Psalm 96:8

113

Harvest Time

Harvest time has come again,
And gathering days are here;
The Autumn leaves are falling,
The Winter's cold is near.
The seeds sown in the springtime
Have turned to yellow grain;
We gather now and store for use
'Til harvest comes again.

The trees will soon be bare and shorn
Of their autumnal coat;
And soon will stand, their leafless forms
Stark, silent, and remote.

But they are only sleeping –
Waiting for the touch of Spring;
Soon back will come the coat of green,
And songbirds on the wing.

Now sow the seeds of truth, my friend,
Ere harvest comes again,
And God will send the sunshine;
He also sends the rain.
When sowing days are over,
And harvest days have come,
He'll gather in the golden grain
To His eternal home.

Nona Mae Coone

*I will give the seasonal rain to your land,
the early rain and the late rain, that you
may have your grain, wine and oil…*
Deuteronomy 11:14

Summer's End

How beautiful is this September morning,
Mellow sunshine falls upon my face,
As I walk along the narrow dirt road;
The countryside is an enchanting place.
Goldenrods nod in the tranquil meadow;
Asters lift their petals toward the sun.
I watch a redbird in the marshy thicket
And marvel at the webs which spiders spun.
Yellow leaves float aimless on the water
Of the pond, now desolate and still.
A little boat tugs gently on its mooring;
While crickets call, relentlessly and shrill.
There are honking sounds behind the treetops –
Canadian geese wing through the cloudless blue;
They circle low above an empty cornfield,
Then one by one, they disappear from view.
Oh, the fleeting beauty of this season.
Precious moments, never meant to stay.
When cold winds sweep and Autumn's splendor's faded,
I'll still recall the magic of this day.

Regina Wiencek

Not Mine to Understand

A butterfly came flitting by
Upon the Autumn breeze;
It scaled the springtime lilac bush
And skirted past the trees.
It glided o'er the arbor, high,
All void of roses, red,
Then o'er the country garden grounds
Where flowers were put to bed.

I marveled at the beauteous wings
Of this Fall butterfly;
I wondered how it knew its course
And how it learned to glide.
But it's not mine to understand
The "hows" and all the "whys"…
'Tis mine to bow in awe before
Creator God, all-wise.

Loise Pinkerton Fritz

God's Golden Treasures

Autumn once again is blazing
With its colors bright and bold,
Such a time of joy and laughter –
Treasures of purest gold.

Fields are abundant with the harvest
Of pumpkins orange and round,
Cobs of corn have fallen
Upon the leafy ground.

The harvest moon is beaming
As owls gather near the barn,
Pheasants and turkeys strut their stuff,
Displaying all their charms.

A dreamy breeze of Autumn
Blows gently on the face,
While the leaves of oaks and maples
Tiptoe about the land with grace.

Sassafras and sumac
Are a few treasures from Autumn's chest,
But, oh, the crimson of the oak tree
Reveals Autumn at its best!

Only a God could've created
Such a rainbow-colored sight,
From goldenrod to gingko's fan
And geese which now take flight!

Linda C. Grazulis

Perception

It's all in how you look at it,
That plays the greatest part,
In learning how to deal with life,
And have a happy heart.
Every day's a challenge,
From beginning to the end,
And each of us must lose before
We are allowed to win.
To understand God calls the shots
Can save us needless pain.
Unless we put Him first, we'll make
The same mistakes again.
His gentle heart supplies us with
All the things we lack,
And when we give our love to Him
...He always gives it back.

Grace E. Easley

Joy Within

There is a spring deep within
And from it bubbles joy.
The pleasure that it brings to us
Can rarely be destroyed.
Joy within is a glorious treasure
And produces pure delight.
It brings a lot of happiness
That brightens up our lives.
Joy flows like a mighty river,
Deep within our souls.
It always lifts our spirits
When we are sad and low
Be thankful for this gift of joy.
God gives it to us to share.
It is an expression of His love
To show us that He cares.
Always spread a little joy
Wherever you may go.
This will project to others
That God dwells in your soul.

Shirley Hile Powell

I Know That He Loves Me

All the stars are twinkling
In the sky above,
The moon softly beaming
With rays of God's love.
Though shadows are creeping,
The night holds no fear
For angels surround me
Thus God is so near.
I bow down before Him
As I kneel in prayer,
I give Him my burdens,
Each heartache and care.

I know I can trust Him,
Thus, with faith complete,
I know that in time, all
My needs He will meet.
I know that He loves me,
That heavenly One,
He proved it the day that
He gave His own Son.
And so as my eyes close
In sweet, peaceful sleep,
The angels will guard me
And His watch He'll keep.

Mary E. Herrington

There's
Something Magic

There's something truly magic
When first soft snowflakes fall,
To blanket all the Winter world –
A cover over all.

A canopy of sparkling white
Within the calm and still,
Such beauty as the stars look down
To light the far-off hill.

'Tis truly something magic
To dress each naked tree,
Each branch is wrapped in splendor
For happy hearts to see.

No footprints on the country lane
To mar the beauty there,
A fairyland of wondrous white
That sparkles everywhere.

The first snowfall of Winter
So truly brings a thrill,
As Autumn slowly slips away
In moments white and still.

Each evergreen is laden down,
Snow drifts along the lane,
There's something truly magic
When Winter smiles again.

Garnett Ann Schultz

Adorn yourself with
grandeur and majesty,
and array yourself with
glory and splendor.
Job 40:10

Winterscape

North winds crisp the morning air
And sculpture the new-fallen snow
Into drifts of glittering diamonds
Jack Frost scattered not long ago.

The landscape is ermine wrapped
In a snowy brilliancy,
Sunlight sparkles this wonderland
Presenting a Winter fantasy.

Icicles cling to frosty eaves,
Leafless trees are wintering;
Then March awakens suddenly –
And Spring comes a-blossoming.

Nora M. Bozeman

All you winds, bless the
Lord; praise and exalt Him
above all forever.
Daniel 3:65

The Picture

Virgin snow so pure and white
Softly covering fields of green;
White crystals sparkling in the light;
Here Nature paints a magical scene.

Look now across a crystal pond;
A mirror for the sky.
See reflections in the water
Of treetops ever so high.

Hidden beneath the fallen snow
Small animals in Winter rest.
Hastily birds fly into the trees
In time to feather their nest.

Everywhere now see beauty in white,
At this picture without a frame –
It's a painting that needs no brush,
By an Artist that needs no name.

William Lovett

*Shout with joy
to the Lord,
all the earth;
break into song;
sing praise.*

Psalm 98:4